# Quit Your Job: Amazon v. eBay

## *Work from Home & Earn from Passive Income – A Guide to Multiple Income Streams*

**By Mark Johnston**

# Table Of Contents

# Introduction

Are you fed up and ready to quit your job?

Do you want to work from home?

Are you interested in generating passive income so you can retire young?

Do you want to learn how to make money online?

If so, congratulations on downloading this book!

*Quit Your Job: Amazon v. eBay* will teach you everything you need to know about how to make money online on these sites. Amazon and eBay are the two most popular sites on the Internet for buying and selling products and even services, with millions of users from all over the world.

In this book you will learn:

- How to make money on Amazon without actually having to sell anything.

- The best way to make money online from eBay, including how to choose the right products to sell and how to create a listing that will entice buyers.

- How to generate passive income by selling your own e-book on the Amazon Kindle Platform.

- How to sell on Amazon in order to get the best results and boost your profits.

- And more!

Thank you again for downloading this book. I hope you enjoy it and that it is useful to you!

This document is geared towards providing exact and reliable information in regards to the topic and issue covered. The publication is sold with the idea that the publisher is not required to render accounting, officially permitted, or otherwise, qualified services. If advice is necessary, legal or professional, a practiced individual in the profession should be ordered.

- From a Declaration of Principles which was accepted and approved equally by a Committee of the American Bar Association and a Committee of Publishers and Associations.

# Chapter 1 Amazon v. eBay – Comparing the Two Marketplaces

When it comes to making money by selling stuff online, there are only two major choices that most sellers consider – Amazon or eBay. While there are other sites where you can sell your stuff – Craigslist or Etsy for example –none have the reach and impact of these two major online marketplaces. To help you decide which one you should use, here is a quick comparison of the two sites.

The one most important difference between the two sites when it comes to making money is that you can make money on Amazon without directly being a seller. By signing up as an Amazon Affiliate, you can direct people to vendors' websites and when they buy something, no matter how small, you will get a commission.

Another difference is that eBay still functions on an auction model – instead of having a fixed price for a product; you can accept bids and sell to the buyer with the highest bid at the end of the auction period, which can be up to ten days. However, there is a "Buy It Now" feature that allows the seller to set a fixed price. This means that the buyer can complete the purchase at once, like a traditional sale.

On the other hand, when you list on Amazon, you set a fixed price for the product you are selling. However, your listing then appears next to new versions of the product sold by Amazon itself, which makes it more competitive since budget-conscious shoppers can choose to buy a used version at a more affordable price rather than paying more for new.

This comparison highlights the major difference in the basic nature of the two sites. While Amazon has a network of sellers, it sells the majority of the products you can find on its site. On the other hand, eBay does not sell any product; instead, it acts as a way for buyers and sellers to connect with each other.

This has led to the general perception that it is better to sell new products on Amazon and old products on eBay. Helping to cement this impression is the fact that Amazon requires sellers to provide a UPC code for every item sold. This would make it more complicated for sellers who are selling unique products.

There is also a difference in the way the two sites facilitate the relationship between buyer and seller. Amazon acts as a middleman between the two parties, receiving the seller's money on his behalf. EBay, in contrast, allows the buyer and seller to work out amongst themselves how the product will be shipped and how payment will be made. Both sites, however, offer seller protection services to reduce the risk of fraud.

## Fee Structure

### eBay

As an individual seller on eBay, you are entitled to (at present) 50 free listings, after which you will have to pay an insertion fee for every additional listing. Once your item is sold, you will pay eBay a flat final value fee of 10% on the selling price.

If you plan to do a lot of selling, you can avail of an eBay stores subscription, which will give you from 200 to 2,500 free listings, depending on your subscription level, as well as an additional 100 free auction-style listings for collectibles and fashion. You are also entitled to lower insertion fees when you go over your free allocation and a lower range of final value fees.

### Amazon

Amazon has a more complex fee structure, which charges a listing fee as well as a referral fee if you are an Individual seller. In addition, there is a variable closing fee for items, which is calculated based on their weight, and a fixed fee for books and other media (DVD and video).

Sellers are allowed to list in some 20 to 30 product categories. In addition, they can avail of the Fulfillment by Amazon service, which stores their products in an Amazon warehouse and then shipped directly to the buyer.

## Listings

### eBay

The site allows you to make customized listings with full-color illustrations. This makes it easier to sell unique items since you can personalize the listings to catch the eye of buyers. In addition, eBay has also introduced a "sell for me" service wherein eBay employees will list and sell the product on your behalf. However, completing the purchase is less convenient since you will have to leave the eBay site to pay through PayPal.

### Amazon

If you are selling a product that is already available on the site, listing is easy since all you have to do is input the UPC or SKU number. This means that you no longer have to include relevant information on the product since it is listed automatically. In addition, completing a purchase is easier since Amazon has "1-click buying" feature that lets you check out without having to leave the site.

## Payment

### eBay

In order to get paid for your sales, you will have to open an account. Your sales will be remitted through PayPal, which charges a transfer fee for depositing money into your account.

Amazon

You set up a seller's account on the site, and your sales are remitted through periodic direct deposit into your bank account. Once you sign up on the site, you are automatically registered for a Professional Account as well as enrolled in the Fulfillment program.

Here are some other quick facts that might be useful:

Active Customer Accounts (as of the fourth quarter 2015):

Amazon – 304 million worldwide

eBay – 162 million worldwide

Demographics:

Amazon (2014) US customers

- Below 20 – 5%
- 21 to 29 – 21%
- 30 to 39 – 25%
- 40 to 49 – 23%
- 50 to 59 – 15%
- Over 60 – 12%

eBay

- 18 to 24 – 14%
- 25 to 34 – 18%
- 35 to 49 – 32%

- 50 to 64 – 29%
- 65 and up – 7%

Sales/Revenues

eBay: $8.59B (fiscal year January to December 2015)

Amazon: $107 B

# Chapter 2 Evolution of Amazon and eBay

One of the most interesting observations about the evolution of Amazon and eBay is the different directions the two online retail sites have taken. While eBay has essentially retained its focus as an online market where buyers and sellers can interact, Amazon has expanded and grown, providing not just a wider range of products but even offering a streaming video service that produces its own content as well as other services such as a housekeeping service, Amazon Home Services, and an e-mail service, WorkMail.

Amazon

Jeff Bezos founded Amazon in the early 1990s after he realized that there were great possibilities in e-commerce as the Internet continued to grow and more and more households were connected to the web. After making a list of products he thought would sell well online, he decided to focus on books. Initially the venture was headquartered in Bezos' garage but quickly moved to an office in its home city of Seattle as the site gained popularity. It was so successful that at the end of its first month of operation, it was already receiving and fulfilling orders from all fifty states and 45 countries overseas.

Amazon also pioneered the practice of dropshipping. Instead of maintaining a large inventory, it took orders and then sourced them from the publisher and wholesaler, shipping them directly to the customer. This meant that the company had low overhead and operations costs, and thus was able to offer substantial discounts of 10% to 30% to its customers.

To further help fuel its growth, Amazon launched its Associates program in 1996, which allowed affiliates with their own website to place ads for particular titles on it. They would then receive a commission for every book purchased by a customer who clicked on the ad from their site.

As the company grew, it not only expanded its reach to other countries by acquiring online booksellers based in Europe and abroad, but also increased their product line. In 1998 it launched an online music store on its site and by 1999 it was also offering kitchenware and patio and lawn furniture, among other products. In addition, Amazon has developed its own house brands – Pike Street, Denali, Strathwood and Pinzon – which sell a wide range of products ranging from bed linens to power chairs, and which are made in ten countries.

It also started offering its own line of consumer electronics, starting with the Kindle ebook reader in 2007, which was followed by the Kindle Fire tablet computer and the Amazon Fire TV. It also released its own smartphone, the Fire Phone, in 2014.

eBay

Pierre Omidyar initially founded the site that would eventually evolve into eBay as a way to help his future wife with her hobby. Pam collected Pez dispensers and traded them with other collectors. But she found it too difficult to find others with the same hobby, so Omidyar started AuctionWeb in Labor Day 1995. His initial concept for the site was as an online bazaar that would allow people with similar interests to sell their collectibles.

For the first few months of its existence, AuctionWeb offered its platform to users for free, slowly building up a community of collectors who learned about it through word of mouth. In 1996, however, Omidyar incorporated AuctionWeb as eBay (for electronic Bay Area) and quit his day job as a software developer so he could devote himself to the site full-time.

eBay changed the whole concept of online auctions by transforming it from a process that was conducted either business-to-consumer or business-to-business, to one in which the sellers and buyers interacted directly. Initially, bidders submitted their bids for a listing through e-mail and were informed when someone else had made a higher bid. This gave them the opportunity to either raise their bids or choose to drop out.

Once a seller accepted a bid, they contacted the buyer and made arrangements for shipping and payment. eBay's role in the process was just to act as a broker, and did not sell any items of its own. The site made money by charging sellers a minimal listing fee plus a small percentage of the selling price.

The simplicity of the site's concept helped make eBay profitable almost from the time it went online. People appreciated not just being able to buy and sell their items simply, but also the promise of being able to meet others with similar interests.

In the face of increasing competition from other sites that were also starting to offer online auctions, eBay started making acquisitions that would strengthen its brand as the premier online auction site. It acquired Krause International, an auctioneer that specialized in collectible cars, and 135-year-old auction house Butterfield, in order to expand into higher-end collectibles.

eBay also acquired Billpoint, a payments solution that allowed buyers to pay for their purchases using credit cards and receive reference reports about their transactions. However, it would eventually close Billpoint after it acquired PayPal in the early 2000s.

In 1999, eBay also started expanding overseas by acquiring the German online trading site Alando de AG. This marked the start of its bid for global domination and it eventually would become one of the biggest online auctioneers in the UK and Germany. eBay is also experiencing booming expansion in Korea and France.

After failed attempts at penetrating the high-end auction market through its eBay Premiere site, eBay has decided to focus on its core business and what people still visit the site for, an easy-to-access marketplace where they can buy and sell products through auctions and fixed-price sales.

# Chapter 3 Making Money as an Amazon Associate

As we mentioned earlier, you don't have to actually sell anything to make money from Amazon; instead, you can earn commissions by directing buyers to the Amazon website through your website or blog. You earn higher commissions (called "advertising fees" by Amazon) depending on the number of products your referees buy as well as the type of product they purchase.

Once you've signed up for an Amazon Associates account, you need to create a link from your site to a particular Amazon page. Doing this is easy since there is a tool bar that appears on top of the page once you've signed in. You also have the option to link to an Amazon search page or the Amazon home page. Note that you will earn commissions from any purchase your referee makes on the site, not just from the page you linked to. Thus, if you linked to a page selling digital cameras and your referee not only bought a camera but also a camera case and extra lenses, you will earn commissions from all of them.

It is important to note, however, that you only qualify for an advertising fee if your referee placed items in their Shopping Cart within 24 hours after they landed on any Amazon.com site. Once this 24-hour period elapses, you will not be eligible for any fees until the customer re-enters

Amazon through one of your links, and a new 24-hour period starts. Even if the customer did not place an order but added items to their Shopping Cart, you still qualify for an advertising fee as long as they placed their order before the end of the expiration period of the Shopping Cart (which is generally around 90 days).

The amount of your commission is computed based on the number of products sold. For general products, the commission starts at 4% but increases to 6% once you've made seven sales. As you make more sales, the amount of your commission increases by 0.5% per tier until it reaches the maximum 8.5% once you've sold 3,131 products. However, at the start of the following month, your commission goes back to the base 4% and you have to start building it up again. The commissions for electrical goods are fixed at 4% and those for digital goods at 10%, no matter the quantity. In addition, computers are fixed at a maximum $25 and instant video and DVD sales are capped at $1.50.

Sales are paid out every sixty days, and you have to reach a minimum $10 in sales if you want to be paid by Amazon gift card or direct deposit, and $100 if you are paid via check. If you fail to make the minimum amount, your sales will be carried over to the following month. For example, if you only made $5 in January, this amount will be carried over onto February and added to any sales you make, and your payment will be remitted in March. Note that your earnings will only be remitted if the customer has bought the item, paid for it in full and accepted delivery.

Thus, there are two strategies you can pursue when making money from Amazon Associates – sell more products or focus on promoting products that have higher commission rates. Fortunately, you have one big advantage on your side and that is Amazon itself and its reputation for providing great products and outstanding customer service.

Once you get a person to click on the Amazon link and visit the site, it is very likely that they will buy something. After all, Amazon is really good at selling. So you should focus your energies on getting your readers to click that Amazon link rather than persuading them to buy something from the site once they get there.

Another important thing to remember is that, while you can make a decent amount of money as an Amazon Associate, it takes time before you start to do so. You will need to first generate a lot of traffic to your site, and then motivate visitors to click on your Amazon link to make a purchase.

Here are some tips on how to increase your earnings as an Amazon Associate:

Stick with your niche. While it can be tempting to direct your referees to products that generate higher commissions, you can get better results by referring them to products related to your site's market niche.

For example, if you are a photography blog that focuses on compact cameras, don't suddenly recommend digital cameras just because you can earn more from them. Your readers might see this as a violation of the trust they have built with you.

Also keep in mind that it is important to remain relevant to your niche. In other words, don't suddenly promote a product that is not related to the subject of your blog. This is a transparent ploy that will only erode your credibility with your readers and make it harder for you to get them to click on your Amazon links.

Content, content, content. Generating good content is the bedrock of any marketing strategy. Content will not only drive traffic to your site, it will also help build a loyal base who will follow your recommendations. So you have to make sure that your content is interesting and useful to your site visitors.

Sell products that are within an average price range. The motivation behind this strategy is that average-priced products are easier to sell than more expensive ones, but will still pay a decent amount in commissions. They are not too expensive that the buyer will have second thoughts but not too cheap you're your earnings will be too low. Choose products that lie within the $150 to $300 range.

At the same time, however, you may want to consider promoting certain high-end products. While these products are guaranteed not to generate high conversion rates, even one sale can net you a high commission if the commission rate is big enough.

Be honest. If you are using product reviews to promote a product, make sure that you have actually used it and write a review that is honest about its strengths and weaknesses. This is particularly important since you want to build credibility with your readers. In addition, you should also keep in mind that you should answer the question: how can this help the reader?

Thus, if you are writing a review of a digital camera, you should not only focus on its features but also on who it is best suited for, i.e. is it good for people who do not have a background in photography but want a camera that will enable them to take superior pictures?

Another important thing to keep in mind is that you should focus your promotion on products that are of high quality. As much as possible, try to promote products that you have actually used and are satisfied with. Otherwise, do your homework and read customer reviews to see which products are worth promoting and linking to.

Focus your promotion efforts during the holidays. Since people have more money to spend at Christmas and are focused on buying gifts for their loved ones, you should start promoting your Amazon links as early as November.

You should also take advantage of Amazon promotions. They have a number of promos to help their affiliates, which they tell them about in emails, as well as on a blog. These deals not only offer discounts to buyers but also give associates bonus commissions for products in particular niches or for certain items. Promote only those that are relevant to your niche.

Also worth keeping an eye for are sales and other deals that they are promoting on certain pages. If they relate to what you are doing on your blog, so should definitely take advantage of them to help boost your commissions.

One way you can increase your sales is by publishing a post with recommendations for gifts, complete with illustrations and honest reviews. Make sure that each item has a link to the relevant Amazon page. You should also include links to related products and accessories to help boost sales further.

Do your keyword research. Choosing the right keywords for your content and your site can be tricky, since you want those that rank well in searches but are not too competitive that you will find it hard to get highly ranked.

In addition, the right keywords are important to generating engaged traffic. Keep in mind that it is more important to your success as an affiliate that you get fewer visitors, but who are genuinely interested in your market niche and what you have to say, than having more traffic, but which consists of casual visitors who are just there to browse and are not interested in engaging with you.

Promote your content using social media. Start a Facebook page, and then promote your new content on your status updates. Open a Twitter account and tweet links to new articles and videos. Doing this will not only increase the amount of traffic you get, but also help improve your click-through and conversion rates.

Offer prizes. You can redeem part of your earnings as an Amazon gift card and then start contests on your site or promote your social media. For example, you can ask people to like your Facebook page and then, when you've reached a certain number of likes, you can raffle off the gift card.

Integrate the links into your content. One of the best ways to encourage people to click on a referral link is by including it as part of an article or blog post. For example, if you have a post about the benefits of juicing, you can mention the particular model of juicer you are using, with the name of the product hyperlinked to its Amazon page.

Focus on 'needs' rather than 'wants'. A lot of people nowadays shop for necessities on Amazon that they would normally have bought from the grocery. In addition, you should promote products that might generate other sales. For example, you can promote baby diapers, knowing that the chances are high that mothers buying these products will also buy other baby necessities.

Focus on products that you can write interesting content on. It is very important that you make your promotion as organic as possible and not seem as if you are 'hard-selling' your readers. Keep in mind that they visited your site to read interesting content, not to be sold to. So don't write content that is a disguised advertisement or obviously written because you are pushing a certain product.

Listen to what your readers want. You can keep in touch with the pulse of your readership by reading the comments sections of your posts and then adjusting your marketing strategy accordingly. Look at what products they are responding to, for instance.

Refresh evergreen content. If you have old content that has been popular with your readers but does not have any Amazon links in it, you can refresh it by updating it. You can then add links to the relevant Amazon pages.

Don't worry about starting early. If you are just starting your blog now, you should not hesitate to sign up for Amazon Associates. Even if you are just building up your readership, you will learn a lot about how to promote your affiliate link. And as your readership grows, your links will continue to convert for years and continue to earn you a recurring income.

# Chapter 4 Making Money Self-Publishing on Amazon Kindle

The success of Kindle and e-books has opened the door for millions of authors to self-publish their books and reach readers directly. In the past, most authors would have to suffer a ton of rejections before they got a book deal with a publisher. Even with a deal, however, there was no guarantee that you would earn money from your book or even that the publisher would market it properly.

Through the Kindle Direct Publishing platform, an author can easily self-publish a book and see it on the site within 24 hours. Self-publishing is free and the platform even allows you to design your own cover. You retain all rights to your work and you are paid a royalty per copy sold based on the price of the e-book. In addition, you set the price of the e-book and manage your sales through your Amazon account. Amazon distributes your books and collects and remits royalties for them.

Although self-publishing was dismissed in the past due to the perception that authors who went this route were of poor quality, these success stories of writers who have self-published on Amazon and reached best-seller status are becoming increasingly common. Louise Ross, who was on maternity leave from the law firm where she worked, wrote a book after giving birth. The resulting novel, Holy Island, has sold more than 70,000 copies and earned its author 70,000 pounds in royalties and has reached the top spot in Kindle's bestseller list.

Of course, not everybody can achieve best-seller status. But if you write a book that reaches an audience, even a niche one, you can earn a decent amount of money. And if enough people continue to buy your books, you might even be able to quit your job and write full-time.

In order for you to earn a decent amount of royalties, your book has to rank in the top 10,000. While this does not seem that difficult, consider that there are hundreds of thousands of self-published books on Kindle. But if you believe that you have something valuable to contribute, there is no reason why you should not reach an audience and break into the top 10,000. Here are some tips to help increase your chances of success when publishing independently on Kindle.

Choose a niche where you can stand out. The worst type of authors are those who chase trends, that is, if the most popular books are erotic thrillers such as Fifty Shades of Grey, then that is what they would write. The writers who do this rarely succeed simply because their heart is not in what they are writing, and readers can usually sense this lack of authenticity. In addition, even if the author is fortunate enough to hit with a book, they are very rarely able to follow it up and sustain their success.

The best way to reach an audience is to find a niche that you are genuinely interested in and write a book about it. At the same time though, it would not hurt to do some market research and see if there is a sufficient audience for your niche that you would be able to sell enough books. You can conduct this research by doing a search for books in your proposed niche in the Kindle Store. Doing this research can also help you find a topic that audiences are genuinely interested in learning about but is underserved, and which you can write a book about.

Make your book look professional. One of the reasons why self-published books have earned a bad reputation in the past was because they looked amateurish. Aside from the quality of the writing being bad, they also had many typographical errors and grammatical mistakes. Before you upload your book, go over it at least twice to eliminate these typos as much as possible.

If you can, you should consider hiring a professional copy editor to go through your book and edit it for you. To help make your book stand out even more, you might also want to hire a designer to create a cover for you, since relying on the templates in the Kindle platform will result in a bland cover.

Price it appropriately. One of the weirdest things about pricing e-books is that people treat them as if they were any other product. Instead of considering the value they are getting, they look at the number of pages in the book and then ask if the price is worth it.

For example, Professor Brian Cox published a short book that explains, in layman's terms, how the universe will end. However, despite distilling a complex subject into just twenty pages, most readers commented that the 99p the publisher was charging was not worth the price because the book was too short.

Marketing, marketing, marketing. One of the hardest aspects of self-publishing is that it is up to you to promote your book. If you have a blog that already has a loyal readership, then this can be simple. All you have to do is sell it directly to your audience. On the other hand, if you are a beginning author with minimal web presence, what can you do?

Social media is an easy and affordable way to find an audience for your book. If you have a Facebook page, you can reach out to your Facebook friends who you know are interested in the topic of your book. You can offer free copies to those who you feel are influential and ask them to recommend it to their friends if they like the book.

You can also consider published a limited number of copies of your book as a paperback through print-on-demand services such as Amazon's CreateSpace. This will hopefully drive sales of both versions, since not everyone is into e-books. You can even sell your print books directly to readers through your site, since you can buy them at cost, allowing you to keep a higher share of the profits.

# Chapter 5 Make Money Selling on Amazon

These days, with an increasing number of people doing their shopping online, there are great opportunities available to you by selling on Amazon. You not only can sell your products on Amazon as one of its network of sellers, but also your services using Amazon Services and even homemade products through Amazon Handmade. At present, according to Amazon, some 40% of its sales come from third-party sellers.

We will only discuss how to sell your products on Amazon in this chapter, since Amazon Services and Amazon Handmade are on an invitation basis only once your application has been accepted.

How to Sell on Amazon

Before you register for an account, you have to check if the product you plan to sell falls into the twenty categories Amazon has opened to third-party sellers. Most of these categories allow you to list products without seeking permission from Amazon; however, others not only require specific permission but you also have to adhere to guidelines such as only being able to list new products or meet other requirements.

Examples of categories that require no permission include Amazon Kindle, Cameras and Photos, Home and Garden, Musical Instruments, Personal Computers, Office Products and Outdoors Products. Categories requiring approval include Watches, Wine, Video Products (including DVDs and Blu-Rays), Shoes, Sunglasses and Handbags and Luggage and Travel Accessories.

Once you've settled on a category and are registering for an account, you need to choose a selling plan. You can choose to be an Individual or a Professional Seller depending on the number of products you intend to sell.

If you will sell no more than 40 products a month, you should register as an Individual Seller since it comes with no monthly subscription fees and you pay $0.99 per item as well as variable closing fees and referral fees.

On the other hand, if you have your own offline store and can sell more than 40 products monthly, you should sign up for a Professional plan. Although you have to pay a monthly fee of $40, you are entitled to list in 30 categories, 10 more than Individual sellers, as well as being exempt from per-item selling fee.

When your account is active, you can use the online interface to start listing your products. If you have an Individual account, you can list your products one at a time, while Professional sellers can list big quantities using bulk tools.

Here are some tips on how you can increase your sales on Amazon:

- Choose unique products that are not currently available on Amazon. This option is only available for sellers that have a Professional account. The major benefits of doing this is that you are marketing to a huge number of potential customers, but at the same time have no competition in your niche. In addition, since there is no competition, you can list the prices at a higher margin.
- List products that have a competitive margin. If you don't have a unique product, then the only way for you to compete on Amazon is through price. Keep in mind that for most shoppers, the main factor determining their buying decision is price, so you have to be able to compete on this basis.
- Use repricing software. This software allows you to stay competitive by monitoring the prices of your competitors

so you can adjust your prices accordingly. In addition, it can help you get into the buy box (the box which appears on the upper right corner of the page and is given to the seller with the lowest price).

- Build a relationship with your customers. In order to help build customer loyalty and hopefully generate repeat business, you can market to them directly. For example, you can offer first-time customers a discount on their next purchase or offer a related product at a reduced price.

- Solicit feedback and reviews from customers. Positive reviews can have a powerful effect on your sales since a majority of consumers say that they enjoy the same level of trust as personal recommendations. If you are offering a new product, contact early buyers and ask them for feedback if they have not left reviews. Or you can offer a 99% discount code to customers in exchange for a review.

- Improve your listings using keywords. Use Amazon's Keyword Search Tool to find long tail keywords that you can use in your title and your keyword fields. Once you've found keywords that you think are appropriate, you can use the Google Keyword Planner Tool to determine their search volume. Use as many keywords as you can in the title of the product to ensure that your product has high rankings when customers do searches. In addition, you should avoid using the same keywords that you use in the title in the keyword field.

- Send readers to your Amazon store. If you have a blog or website, you can use it to promote your products, the same way you would as an Amazon Associate. However, you should be careful when promoting your own products to avoid alienating your readers. Keep your tone friendly and avoid hard selling by hyping the product too much. Instead just act as if you are introducing something to a friend of family member.
- Check how easy it is to find your product. Try this experiment: enter your storefront and listings as if you were a buyer, then look at them from this perspective. Did you have a hard time finding your listing? Is the product description easily understandable and complete? Are the images clear and do they represent the product accurately?
- Use Fulfillment by Amazon. If you are a Pro seller, you should consider using this service for your most popular products in order to increase sales. Fulfillment lets you store your products at an Amazon warehouse and also ship and pack them, as well as providing after-sales services. In addition, FBA allows you to sell to Amazon Prime subscribers, which can greatly help improve your sales

performance since they generate 17% of Amazon's sales, although they only make up some 6% of buyers on the site.

# Chapter 6 Make Money Selling on eBay

EBay has become the site of choice for people who have distinctive items that they want to sell, whether it be old comics or rare collectibles. When you list your items on eBay, you have access to some 100 million buyers, which increases the chances that you will find someone who wants to buy what you have to sell.

As we mentioned earlier, one of the biggest benefits to using eBay is that it costs nothing to list your product, since individual sellers are entitled to 50 free listings a month, and you are only charged a fee when your product is sold. If you plan to set up an online business, it is also very affordable to set up an eBay Store, since the monthly cost can be as low as $19.95 or even less if you have a yearly subscription.

In addition, eBay offers a range of services that can make selling easier, particularly if you are offering products online for the first time. For example, if you don't know how much to charge for your time, you can ask the site to price it for you based on what other sellers are offering.

If you are not sure how to sell, you can avail of the eBay Valet service, which will do all the work for you and you can even ship your products to eBay using prepaid shipping. Once the item is sold you can earn from 60% to 80% of the selling price. And to make shipping to your buyer easier, and to shorten payment times, you can print shipping labels through My eBay.

If you've decided that you want to make money on eBay, the first step is to decide what to sell. It is important for you to find products that will sell well enough to generate a decent recurring passive income for you, while at the same time not entering into a niche that is too competitive and which has too many sellers already. Here are some guide questions to ask:

- What am I interested in? The most effective sellers are those who sell products that they are genuinely passionate about, because they can communicate this enthusiasm to their sellers. In addition, you can create more detailed listings that will demonstrate to interested buyers that you genuinely know what you're talking about. What hobbies do you currently have or had when you were younger. Look at those interests in order to find products that you can sell.
- What products would be helpful to people in a certain niche? If you are currently employed, ask yourself: what are the products that are most useful to people in my profession? You can market these products to others in your field that might need them.
- What products would make my life easier? Sit down and think about a problem or

situation that you recently faced. Then think about a product that would have solved the problem. You can sell these products to people in the same situation as you.

- If all else fails, you can avail of the Marketplace Research service offered by eBay. Powered by Terapeak, the service provides you with access to a wide range of sales data including average selling prices, best performing categories and keywords and market demand for particular products. In addition, once you've found the best-selling products on the site, you are provided with sourcing information for Alibaba products so that you can avail of them at wholesale prices. A free trial is available after which you can subscribe to the service at a low monthly price.

Once you've decided on the products you want to sell, you have to decide how much you will price the item for. The price should be competitive while still allowing you to earn a profit and not lose money on the transaction. If you would like to do your own pricing rather than relying on eBay recommendations, here are some tips:

- Research what similar products are going for. This is the most basic way to decide what a fair price for the item is. You can use eBay's Advanced Search function to search for listings of similar products that have already been sold as well as those that are still active.

- Include the shipping charge in the price. A buyer might decide to go with your item over one that is priced cheaper as long as the combined price with shipping is overall lower.

- Set a reserve price. You can do this for items that you have listed auction-style, in order to ensure that you get a fair price when the item sells. A reserve price is a minimum price that is hidden from the bidder. You can start by listing the item at a low price to generate interest. As long as the reserve price is not reached, a "Reserve not met" notice will appear. The item will only be sold once bidding hits the reserve price.

The next step after pricing is to make an attractive listing for your items. Here are some guidelines to follow:

Write a clear title. You are allowed to use up to 80 characters in your title. Make sure that you include descriptors such as the brand, model number, size, color and condition. Also include keywords that buyers might be searching for so that they can find your listing more easily.

Write a helpful description. The description should provide all the information the buyer might be interested in about the product. For example, what features does it have? When and where was it manufactured? Who designed it? In addition, make sure you clearly state the condition of the item, including any repairs or alternations that were made to it as well as packaging information and other accessories or extras included with the product. To make it easier to read, you can format the description using bullets.

After you write the description read through it again and make sure that you have corrected any typographical errors and grammatical mistakes. The description should also be clearly understandable and easy to read.

If you are selling a single item, but which has variations in features such as size and color, you can save time and effort by creating just one listing for the products using the listings with variations feature.

Include photos. You are allowed to include up to 12 photos with most listings and you should take full advantage of it. To ensure that the photos display your item in the most accurate and attractive way possible, you should take the picture against a plain neutral or white background and using Medium or High file size settings on your camera.

In addition, the item should occupy most of the frame, with as little empty space as possible. Take shots of the product from multiple angles and include several close-up shots that will display its details. Also make sure you show as much of the product as possible. For example, if you are selling a handbag, you should also include photos of the interior.

If you are selling a used product, you should also show any wear and tear the item has, so that the buyer will be fully informed and know what to expect when it arrives.

Finally, the photos should be from 800 to 1600 pixels so that the zoom/enlarge feature is enabled on the product's View page.

If you have a product that you think will be popular, you can consider listing it globally. By doing so, you are significantly expanding your base of potential buyers since your listing will appear on international eBay sites as well as being visible to buyers who are visiting the site from outside the US.

You can either choose the option of creating a separate listing for the eBay site of another country or upgrading to international site visibility listings. If you choose the latter option, you will have to pay a separate fee for each country that you want your listing to be visible in when buyers do searches.

Here are some other tips that can help increase your chances of success as an eBay seller:

- Make sure you keep your inventory stocked. One of the things you most want to avoid is running out of stock of a product that is selling well. So keep track of your inventory and restock when it is already getting low.
- Consider bundling similar items together. If you are selling shoes, for example, you can bundle cleaning items such as a brush and call it a gift package. This might make it more attractive to buyers who will feel that they are getting a higher value for their money.
- Provide a good customer experience. Once you receive the order, make sure that you send out an acknowledgment email to the buyer. Then, once the payment has been received, ship the item as soon as possible and send an email to the buyer informing them that you have done so. It is these little things that will help you build a relationship with your buyer and improve repeat business.
- If you are selling used electronics and appliances, make sure that you include any instruction manuals and related material, if they are still available.
- Make sure that any terms and conditions are listed clearly in the listing. For example, you should clearly include details about shipping times, your return policy and any other important business details. This will help to improve the

buyer's confidence in dealing with you since you are clearly not trying to hide anything from them.

- Use social media to market your eBay listings. If you have a store, you can set up a business page for it on Facebook where you can include status updates on new products and deals that you are offering. You can also tweet links to your eBay listings to your followers. And if you have a blog, you can also write posts about the items you are selling that can provide more information to interested buyers and make it more likely that they will avail of the item.

- If you have an auction listing, time it so that it ends on a Sunday evening. The reason for this is that visitors to the eBay site seem to peak during this time, making it more likely that you will find a buyer. So time your auction so it will end between 8:00 Eastern and 10:00 Pacific. In addition, the period of your auction should be around seven days since it is more convenient to remember. However, this is not a fixed rule and you might decide that a 10-day auction would give you better results by allowing more buyers to see your listing and make bids on it.

# Conclusion

Thank you again for downloading this book!

I hope this book was able to teach you everything you need to know about how to make money online from Amazon and eBay.

The next step is to start practicing what you've learned from this book to make money. Who knows? If you start early enough, then you might even be able to generate multiple income streams from both sites and earn enough to retire early.

If you enjoyed this book, then I'd like to ask you for a favor. Would you be kind enough to leave a review for this book on Amazon? It would help others who might benefit from it find the book more easily. It'd be greatly appreciated!

Finally, thank you and good luck!